THE POLISH TRIVIA BOOK

John M. Vraniak

D1522448

Avenue Publishing Co.
Hamtramck, Michigan 48212

This book is dedicated to:

Christyn L. Harris and Mark Vraniak
. . . and your spirit for living.

also,

Dad — for your courage to venture
to America back in `32.

FOREWORD

I didn't know a Polish man invented Bagels. I was surprised to find out Madame Curie was Polish. Nor was I aware of the important role Poles had in the American Revolutionary War. But I do know most Americans (including Polish-Americans) are not aware of these facts either. And why should they? Polish history isn't taught in most schools. Polish books found in most bookstores are likely to be joke books. One could go to a local library and find a handful of books about Polish history, but most of them are text books. That's why I wrote THE POLISH TRIVIA BOOK.

My friend hit the nail on the head when he described THE POLISH TRIVIA BOOK as the "fast food approach" to learning about the Polish and Polish-American experience. After surveying people of various ethnic backgrounds, it was determined the following ingredients would make this book different from any other books on Polish history:

(1) Covertly educate the reader. (This is accomplished by coming up with the right blend of educational facts and trivia.)

(2) Present a good cross-section of subject matter (history, sports, art, literature, food, tradition, language, music, proverbs and more).

(3) Use a question-answer format.

(4) Let the reader find the answers quickly and easily. Even allow the reader to "cheat" if he or she wants to. (You will always find questions on left hand pages and the respective answers on right hand pages.)

(5) Make the book enjoyable to read!

After the readers' wants were defined, all it took was twelve months of free time to research the material and a lot of patience from my wife.

I thank the following individuals (of various ethnic backgrounds) for providing the resources, insight and perspectives to THE POLISH TRIVIA BOOK:

Gene Barnes, Delphine (Nogafski) Bartle, Marvin Bartle, Eddie Blazonczyk, JoAnn and Roger Bonahoom, Cass and Sylvia Cichy, Ron Chapiewski, Don and Ruth Dickie, Sue Dengiz, Ann Fletcher (American Polish Engineering Association), William and Lena Gianino, JoAnn Goble, Pat and Teresa Harris, Kurt Hartwig, Jo Hassell, Barbara (Counsman) Hile, Judy (Pilzner) Judge, Al Judge, Chet Kapla, Ruth and Gar Laity, William Lemieux, Kim and Gary Lennon, Daryl Olszeski, Greg Ozimek, Bill and Nina Rich, Frank and Mary Ann Rizzo, Carl and Laurie Rutkowske, John Skomra, Marie Tatar, Bill and Myrtle Tolstedt, John J. Tosch III, John and Bertha Vraniak (Dad and Mom), Donald Wawrowski, Robert Westerkamp, Glenn Whitelaw and Robert Zahon.

A special thank you to my wife Annette — without her as a sounding board, this project would never have taken off.

I hope you, the reader, will enjoy reading THE POLISH TRIVIA BOOK as much as I did writing the book. If after reading THE POLISH TRIVIA BOOK, you want to take issue with any of the information presented, or want to share information with me for future editions, I want to hear from you. Write to me in care of:

Avenue Publishing Co.
P.O. Box 34301
Detroit, MI 48234

Until then, na zdrowie (nah ZDROH-vee-eh), or to your very good health!

John M. Vraniak

1   QUESTIONS

001   In 1619, Poles in Jamestown made the first civil liberty protest in America after being denied the right to vote, because they were not what?

002   Polish-Americans were attracted to Hamtramck, Michigan in 1914 after the opening of which automobile plant?

003   The first marriage performed in the first Polish Catholic Church in America (in 1854) was for people of what descent?

004   About what percentage of Polish-American congressmen have been democrats?
(A) 25   (B) 50   (C) 75

005   This wide-receiver for the New Orleans Saints led the NFL in pass receptions in 1969?

006   This White House official of the early 1970s, often referred to Poles as "Polacks."

007   In 1898, a group of women met in Chicago and became the Polish:
(A) Pipers   (B) Pilgrims   (C) Alliance of America

008   Polish-American Henryk Arctowski (1871-1958) explored what frigid zone?

001   Of British descent. (They called a strike and won their rights.)

002   Dodge Main

003   Spanish. (The Poles decided the church should serve Spanish people in Texas as well as Polish-Americans.)

004   C

005   Dan Abramowicz

006   Spiro T. Agnew

007   C

008   Antartic. (South Pole.)

3   **QUESTIONS**

009   Surnames ending in "wicz" are typically Polish.
        True or False

010   To distinguish themselves from the commoners, the
        Polish aristocracy adapted the "ski" ending to their
        surnames in the 15th century. True or False

011   Many Polish immigrants added the "ski" ending to their
        names on the ship across the Atlantic.
        True or False

012   The Polish peasantry first adapted the "cki" ending to
        their surnames between 1350 and 1450.
        True or False

013   The Polish Daily News (Dziennik Polski), the major
        Polish-language newspaper still alive today, began
        publication in 1904 in what U.S. city.

014   Approximately 1000 Poles served in the Continental
        Army during which war?

015   All of the 6000 Poles who participated in the Civil War
        fought for the Union. True or False

016   A new dynasty was established in 1386 by a grand duke
        named Jagiello, who became king Wladyslaw II of
        Poland. What nationality was he?
        (A) Polish   (B) Austrian   (C) Lithuanian

009   True

010   True. (But the peasants rebelled and also added "ski" to their names.)

011   True. (They regarded the "ski" as a badge of honor.)

012   False. (First done by Polish nobility.)

013   Detroit

014   American Revolutionary War

015   False. (About 1000 fought for the Confederacy.)

016   C

5   QUESTIONS

017   What Polish-American actress once said, "If you want anything, all you have to do is whistle."?

018   This female celebrity changed her name from Karolina Piekarska to what?

019   What was the nickname of Jane Bartkowicz, one of the world's top tennis players of the 1960s?

020   Steve Bartkowski, the quarterback from California, was the NFLs No.1 draft pick in 1975. Name the team.
(A) Green Bay   (B) Atlanta   (C) New Orleans

021   A surname with a "vic" or "vich" ending is usually Polish. True or False

022   A surname having an "enko" ending is typically Polish. True or False

023   A last name ending in "sky" is typically Polish.
True or False

024   Polish immigrants, more than any other group, changed their names for what major reason?

017   Lauren Bacall. (She was born Betty Perske.)

018   Carroll Baker

019   "Peaches." (Her younger sister, Chris "Plums", also played tennis.)

020   B

021   False. (Yugoslavian)

022   False. (Ukrainian; means son of.)

023   False. (Russian)

024   To simplify spelling and pronounciation. (Some did it to gain social prestige and to avoid ridicule.)

025   What was the highest rank attained by an officer of Polish descent during the Civil War?

026   During which war did the "Polish Brigade" and the "Polish Legion" see significant action in the Virginia and Gettysburg campaigns?

027   What president, in his speech to the Senate on January 22, 1917, supported "a united, independent and autonomous Poland"?

028   The year 1643 saw the first evidence of Polish settlement in New Amsterdam. What was this city later named?

029   Polish-American Miecyslaw Bekker was responsible for developing which vehicle?   (A) Ford Thunderbird (B) Moon Rover   (C) First Helecopter

030   Chuck Bednarik, from the University of Pennsylvania, was the NFLs No.1 draft pick by Philadelphia in 1949. Name his offensive position.

031   This Polish-American was born Patricia Andrezewski, but her Rock 'n' Roll fans know her as whom?

032   Bruce Bialaski, who called himself a "Lithuanian of Poland", was which organization's first director? (A) YMCA   (B) AFL-CIO   (C) FBI

025   Brigadier-General. (Albin Schoepf of the Union Army.)

026   Civil War

027   Woodrow Wilson. (Polish and Polish-American agitation helped create his declaration.)

028   New York City

029   B. (Used in Appollo space program.)

030   Center

031   Pat Benatar

032   C. (From 1912 to 1919.)

033   In terms of numbers, where do Polish-Irish marriages rank in Polish-America?

034   In terms of numbers, where do Polish-Italian marriages rank in Polish-America?

035   In terms of numbers, where do Polish-German marriages rank in Polish-America?

036   Polish-Chinese, Polish-Filipino, and Polish-Korean marriages happen most frequently in what state?

037   In 1868, the first Polish school in America was established at St.Stanislaus Parish in which city?
(A) Milwaukee   (B) Buffalo   (C) Detroit

038   In 1795, Poland was partitioned for the third time by Austria, Prussia and Russia. It disappeared as an independent state until what year?

039   During their massive immigrations of the 19th century, the majority of Polish immigrants worked as farmers.
True or False

040   The Poles brought with them to the U.S., a passionate love of freedom and a burning desire to own what?

033   First

034   Second

035   Third

036   California

037   A

038   1918

039   False. (Common laborers in factories, steel mills and mines.)

040   Land

041   What late actor portrayed Bluto Blutarski in the 1978 hit film, "National Lampoon's Animal House"?

042   Karol J. Bobko was the first Polish-American: (A) Astronaut   (B) Hockey Player   (C) Pizza Maker

043   Craig Bodzianowski gained national recognition in 1985 after he lost his right leg in a motorcycle accident and resumed his career in what profession?

044   Vince Boryla was an All-American at both Notre Dame and Denver Universities before playing two decades as a pro in what sport?

045   Marriages between Polish-Americans and American Indians are most frequent in what state?

046   Kowalski-Goldstein marriages are most common in what U.S. city?

047   Name one of the seven most common surnames in Warsaw, Poland.

048   In Poland, when a woman marries, she takes her husband's surname and changes the last letter to what?

041   John Belushi

042   A. (Also piloted a space shuttle.)

043   Boxing

044   Basketball. (1940s, 1950s)

045   North Dakota

046   New York

047   Dabrowski, Kaminski, Kowalski, Nowak, Szymanski, Wisniewski and Zielinski.

048   An "a". (Example: Mr. Wolinski's wife would be Mrs. Wolinska.)

049   In 1890, what percent of America's total Polish population lived in cities and towns around the Great Lakes?   (A) 25   (B) 50   (C) 80

050   In 1608, Polish immigrants built the first furnace in America for making: (A) Glass   (B) Bread   (C) Steel

051   Which one of the following cities does **not** have sizable Polish-American populations?   (A) New York (B) Cleveland   (C) Memphis   (D) Milwaukee

052   Which one of the following cities does **not** have sizable Polish-American populations? (A) Cincinnati   (B) Buffalo   (C) Detroit   (D) Pittsburgh

053   In 1843, Poland's Countess Rosa Branicka rejected medical opinions that she was suffering from cancer. She (by herself) surgically removed a tumor from what part of her body?

054   What man is best remembered as Bart Starr's back-up quarterback at Green Bay from 1963-68?

055   This actor was born Charles Buchinski.

056   Lydia Bruce spent 15 years as Dr. Maggie Powers on what NBC Emmy Award-winning soap opera?

049   C

050   A

051   C

052   A

053   Breast

054   Edmund "Zeke" Bratkowski

055   Charles Bronson

056   "The Doctors."   (Born Lydia Slubowska.)

057   Polish people will sometimes call a man "Stash" if he has what first name?

058   The Polish surnames Taback or Tabachnick were originally given to a man who indulged in what item he prepared and sold?

059   During the name-giving period of Poland, Kowal and Kowalski were the most common surnames and were given to people with what occupation?

060   The Polish surname Stopka was originally given to a man who drank, and perhaps overindulged, what liquor?

061   From 1870 to 1900, approximately how many millons of Poles came to the U.S.?

062   The 1920 U.S. Census reported how many millions of citizens were of Polish descent?

063   Polish immigrants accompanied what famous frontiersman in helping to establish the first settlement in Kentucky?

064   In 1735, immigrant Jan Sadowski became the first white man to cross which mountain range?
A) Rockies   (B) Alleghenies   (C) Smokies

057   Stanley or Stanislaus

058   Snuff. (These names probably originated in the 16th century when tobacco was first introduced to Europe.)

059   Smith. (Slotnick was a goldsmith.)

060   Vodka

061   One

062   Three

063   Daniel Boone

064   B

065   Jimmy Carter's White House staff called this man "Woody Woodpecker" because Woody is easier to pronounce than Zbigniew.

066   Fred Bujack is a member of what sport's Hall of Fame?

067   Bill Burke is a member of what sport's Hall of Fame?

068   This Polish-American comedian was born Aaron Chwatt in 1919 but is known to millions today as whom? [He got his nickname from his once full head of red hair.]

069   The Polish surnames Yablonski or Jablonowski were originally given to men who lived near what kind of tree?

070   The Polish surname Karpinski was originally given to a man who caught what kind of fish?

071   The Polish surnames Sadowski and Sadecki were originally given to men who had something to do with what?   (A) Orchards   (B) War   (C) Liquor

072   The Polish surname Flaska was originally given to one who made what for a living?

065 Zbigniew Brzezinski. (As National Security Advisor, he was the first American of Polish birth to attain Cabinet level status.)

066 Bowling

067 Golf. (Born Bill Burakowski.)

068 Red Buttons

069 Apple. (Dulski grew pears.)

070 Carp

071 A

072 Little flasks and bottles

073   In 1608, the first Polish immigrants distilled tar and pitch, and erected what type of mill?
(A) Wind   (B) Flour   (C) Saw

074   Poles, early on, provided the bulk of labor in Chicago's:
(A) Slaughterhouses   (B)Auto Factories   (C) Construction Industry

075   Early on, Poles provided the bulk of labor for what two industries in Pittsburgh?

076   From 1870 on, the Poles who entered the U.S. (by hundreds of thousands) were skilled professionals.
True or False

077   What U.S. president visited Poland in 1977, and left a memorable first impression?

078   When Frederic Chopin, the infamous 19th century Polish composer, died, which of his organs was sent to his native Poland for burial?

079   In 1979, the Rev. Leonard Chrobot (KRO-bott) helped found a national organization to promote mutual understanding and respect among Polish-Americans and _____-Americans.

080   Konstantin Ciolkowski (1857-1935) is known as the "Father of Modern _____".
(A) Rocketry   (B) Medicine   (C) Refrigeration

073   C

074   A

075   Steel and Coal

076   False. (Poor peasants.)

077   Jimmy Carter. (He told a large welcoming crowd, through an official State Department translator, "I am pleased to be grasping your secret parts.")

078   Heart. (The rest of his body was buried in Paris.)

079   Jewish. (The Polish-American / Jewish-American National Dialog.)

080   A

081   If your surname were Bartkiewicz or Bartkowski, it would be equivalent to what English name?

082   If your surname were Sienkiewicz or Szymanski, it would be equivalent to what English name?

083   During the name-giving period of Poland, a man from Krakow would be named what?

084   The Polish surname Kukulka was originally given to a person named after what bird?

085   Prior to 1870, most Polish refugees were cultured professional men who soon found employment in skilled U.S. professions. True or False

086   The U.S. repaid its Polish heroes by opening the gates to exiled Polish patriots after unsuccessful revolts within their country in 1830, 1848 and 1863. True or False

087   In 1939, Germany joined hands with what country in conquering and dividing Poland?

088   On July 31, 1944, Polish underground forces rose up and almost regained control of Warsaw from the Nazis. Soon afterward, Warsaw was taken by the troops of what country?

081   Bartholomew

082   Simon

083   Krakowski or just Krakow

084   Cuckoo

085   True

086   True

087   U.S.S.R.

088   U.S.S.R.

089   A Polish woman was the personal dialogue coach for this actor when he played Morris Townsend in the 1949 motion picture, "The Heiress."   (A) Montgomery Clift   (B) Clark Gable   (C) Errol Flynn

090   What Polish astronomer was the first to discover that the Earth and its fellow planets revolve around the sun?

091   Harry Coveleski was nicknamed "The Giant Killer." What was his occupation?

092   John Crimmins thrilled fans as a top competitor for four decades as a:
(A) Bowler   (B) Softball Pitcher   (C) Wrestler

093   The Polish surname Yaworski was originally given to one living near what kind of tree?

094   The Polish surname Muchnick was originally given to a man who was as little and unimportant as a what?

095   The Polish surnames Babiarz and Gach were originally given to men who were extremely fond of what from women?

096   During the name-giving period of Poland, what surname was given to a man who was considered old-womanish and lacking masculinity?

089   A

090   Nicolaus Copernicus. (1473-1543; He was also first to discover that the Earth rotates on its axis.)

091   Baseball Pitcher. (This southpaw had three consecutive 20-win seasons (1914-16). His brother, Stan, is in Baseball's Hall of Fame.)

092   A. (Born John Krzyminski.)

093   Sycamore. (Dombrowski lived among oaks; Osinski lived among aspens.)

094   Fly

095   Sexual Favors. (It's not known whether these people were approved of.)

096   Baba. (With many variant spellings.)

097   World War II broke out September 1, 1939 with what country's invasion of Poland?

098   Persecuted Catholics from what country in the United Kingdom came to settle in Poland during the 1700s?

099   Demonstrations and strikes by Poles seeking economic justice in the coal fields of Pennsylvania encouraged what union to organize the new immigrants in 1897?

100   What religious order of sisters arrived in the U.S. in 1874 and went on to become the largest and most important Polish sisterhood in America?

101   Born Marie Sklodowska in 1867, she married a Frenchman and received the nickname "Madame."

102   Stanley "Zbyszko" Cyganiewicz was the last great undefeated American and World Champion in the classic Greco-Roman style of what?

103   Name the largest Polish-American newspaper, founded by John Dende.

104   What do Polish-Americans John Dingell, Barbara Mikulski and Clement Zablocki have in common?

097   Germany

098   Scotland

099   United Mine Workers

100   The Felician Sisters

101   Marie Curie. (She co-discovered radium, used in cancer treatment, and polonium, used to run heart pacemakers.)

102   Wrestling. (Voted Most Popular Athlete of 1920s. Also spoke eleven languages.)

103   Pol-Am Journal

104   All were elected to congress.

105   During Poland's name-giving period, surnames were never descriptive of peoples' good qualities.
True or False

106   During Poland's name-giving period, surnames were never descriptive of hair color. True or False

107   The Polish surname Figurski was originally given to a man having a handsome what?

108   The Polish surname Kluka was originally given to a man having a big what?

109   Most Polish-Americans supported Theodore Roosevelt, the Republican candidate, in the presidential campaign of 1904. True or False

110   SS. Cyril and Methodius Seminary is the only Polish Seminary in North America. In what state is it located?

111   Who enacted the Displaced Persons Act in 1948 allowing 152,000 Poles, displaced by war, to enter the U.S.?   (A) President Truman   (B) Congress
(C) Supreme Court

112   In 1772, Russia, Prussia and Austria seized one-third of Poland's territory. This is known as the: (A) First Partition   (B) Second Partition   (C) Third Partition

105 False. (Geniusz was intelligent. Spiewak sang well. Glombicki was wise and learned.)

106 False. (Czarnicki was dark, brown, black, brunette, etc. Belofski was blond. Czerwonka had red hair.)

107 Body

108 Nose. (Gembala had a big mouth and Homolka had long legs.)

109 True

110 Michigan. (Founded on Detroit's East Side in 1885 by Rev. Joseph Dabrowski. It is now part of the Orchard Lake Schools in Orchard Lake, Michigan.)

111 B. (President Truman took several steps leading up to this.)

112 A

113   This part Polish football coach reportedly once told his players in his postgame speech: "Let's say the Lord's Prayer and get the hell out of here."

114   In 1985, Joe Dudek, a running back for Plymouth State College (New Hampshire) set a NCAA record for most career what?

115   In 1961, Polish-American Dr. Stanley Dudrick developed I.V.H., a new method of:
(A) Vein Feeding   (B) Birth Control   (C) Testing I.Q.

116   Where are mountains named after the astrophysicist Wladislaw Dziewulski (1878-1964)?

117   The National Polish-American Sports Hall of Fame and Museum is located in the Dombrowski Fieldhouse on the campus of what college?

118   Which of these American League baseball teams do not celebrate Polish-American Night once a year?
(A) Chicago   (B) Detroit   (C) Oakland

119   What major league baseball team celebrates Polish-American Night each year with the presentation of new members into the Polish-American Sports Hall of Fame?

120   What Polish city is Michigan's potato capital?

113   Mike Ditka. (He led his Chicago Bears to victory in the 1986 Super Bowl.)

114   Touchdowns (79)

115   A. (I.V.H. stands for Intravenous Hyperalimentation.)

116   On the moon.

117   St. Mary's College.   (Founded in 1973 by Edmond Browalski in Orchard Lake, Michigan .)

118   C

119   Detroit Tigers

120   Posen

121 Most Polish people leaving for America during the 1800s departed from port cities in what country?

122 In his campaign for the presidency in 1960, John F. Kennedy won what percentage of the vote in major Polish-American populations?
(A) 40   (B) 60   (C) 80

123 What U.S. president, in 1970, held two meetings with Polish-American organizations, promising to appoint more qualified Polish-Americans to high federal offices?

124 Slavic tribes in Poland were united by the Piast Dynasty during what century?

125 What U.S. president won 37% of the vote in areas with major concentrations of Polish-Americans in his successful bid to be re-elected in 1956?

126 At what Big Ten school did football coach Forest Evashevski hold the record for career victories (52) before Hayden Fry broke it in 1986?

127 Name the Polish-Jewish immigrant who was originally a make-up man in the early days of motion pictures before becoming a well known cosmetics manufacturer.

128 The writings of this Polish nun were banned by the Vatican in 1958 after she documented her visions of Christ.

121   Germany. (Hamburg and Bremen.)

122   C

123   Richard Nixon

124   9th

125   Dwight Eisenhower

126   University of Iowa

127   Max Factor

128   Sister Faustina.   (Born Helen Kowalska, Pope John
         Paul II persuaded the Vatican to lift the ban in 1978.)

129   One who comes from the Polish community of
           Hamtramck, Michigan is a:
           (A) Hamtramckan (B) Hamtramcker (C) Hamtramckian

130   In 1986, Kowalski Sausage Co., of Hamtramck, Mich-
           igan, created the world's heaviest kielbasa. How many
           pounds did it weigh?
           (A) 546   (B) 1125   (C) 2208

131   In 1985, Kowalski Sausage Co., of Hamtramck, Mich-
           igan, created the world's longest kielbasa. How many
           feet long was it?   (A) 150   (B) 363   (C) 600

132   On September 7, 1977, Phil Nowicki of Rogers City,
           Michigan broke the Guinness World Record for having
           the largest what?

133   The Polish-American Congress, in 1970, joined forces
           to continue official funding for what program that
           broadcasts on radio behind the Iron Curtain?

134   Twelve Polish-Americans were elected to the 87th
           Congress in 1960 — the largest number to that time.
           How many were Democrats?

135   In 1948, Polish-Americans continued to support the
           Democratic party, voting heavily in favor of what pres-
           idental candidate?

136   In the 1950s, Polish-Americans tended to vote for what
           political party?

129   A. (All were used in the early years but this one endured over time.)

130   C. (32-feet long and 15 inches around; cost was approx. $7000.)

131   C

132   Sausage. (8,773 feet long and 1.5 tons in weight.)

133   Radio Free Europe. (Was done over the objections of the Senate Foreign Relations Committee.)

134   Ten

135   Harry Truman

136   Republican

137   William Filene, a Polish immigrant, founded this Boston department store, famous for its bargain basement.

138   This actress and her political activist husband traveled to Poland in 1987 to meet with Solidarity leader Lech Walesa.

139   What Polish-American woman, in 1977, wrote the bestselling novel, <u>The Women's Room</u>?

140   Polish-American Casimir Funk is best remembered as the "Father of:
(A) Polish Radio"   (B) The Corvair"   (C) Vitamins"

141   What model of car was sold through the first Polish-American car dealership in 1913?

142   Carl Rohwetter founded which publication in 1970?
(A) <u>Polish Daily News</u>   (B) <u>The Polish Tabloid</u>
(C) <u>The Polka News</u>

143   Bronski Beat is a:
(A) TV Crime Show   (B) Dance Step   (C) Rock Group

144   A "Polish Opening" and a "Polish Defense" are strategies used in what game?

137   Filene's

138   Jane Fonda and Tom Hayden

139   Marilyn French

140   C. (Not only did he discover vitamins, he was a specialist in deficiency diseases, such as scurvy, pellagra and rickets.)

141   Buick. (Sold by Krajenke Buick located in Hamtramck, Michigan.)

142   C. (Published from his home in St. Charles, Michigan.)

143   C. (Led by Steve Bronski, this band earned raves for its 1985 debut album "The Age of Consent".)

144   Chess

145   As of 1987, how many people of Polish descent live in metropolitan Detroit?
        (A) 200,000   (B) 800,000   (C) 1,500,000

146   The second generation of Poles in America were the first to be born in the United States. True or False

147   If a European heard a Polish joke, he or she would probably find it amusing. True or False

148   During World War II, the Germans murdered 6 million Poles, of which how many million were Jews?

149   When Leo Gerstenzang, a Polish immigrant, noticed his wife using a toothpick covered with cotton to clean between their baby's skin folds, he invented what?

150   Tom Gola, the All-American basketball forward of the 1950s, set a college record for the most what?
        (A) Rebounds   (B) Points   (C) Assists

151   This Polish-Jewish-American ran for president of the United States in 1964.

152   This Polish-born former glove salesman is the 'G' in MGM.

145   B

146   True

147   False. (Probably could not relate to it.)

148   Three

149   Q-Tip Cotton Swabs (1926)

150   A. (Regarded as the greatest player in LaSalle College history.)

151   Barry Goldwater. (His grandfather, Michael Goldwasser, translated his own surname and changed it to Goldwater.)

152   Samuel Goldwyn (1882-1974). (Originally named Gelbfisch, this movie producer translated and changed it to Goldfish and changed it again to Goldwyn.)

153   Invented in 1730 by a French officer and a Polish gentlemen, this game is played on a board of 100 squares (not 64) and each player has 20 pieces (not 12).

154   According to the 1980 U.S. Census, there were about how many million Polish-Americans?

155   When today's top pickle packer started in this business in the 1930s, it sold pickles imported from Poland. Name the company.

156   When Polish and other ethnic jokes first started, they were take-offs on the "Moron Jokes" of what decade?

157   U.S. Census reports starting in 1860 did not give proper credit to the people of Polish parentage.   True or False

158   In the 1800s, significant numbers of Poles arrived in which of the following cities?   (A) Philadelphia (B) Baltimore   (C) Charleston   (D) All of the Above

159   For what war did Polish-Americans sacrifice more lives and give more money than any other single ethnic group in the U.S.?

160   When Polish-Americans, and other immigrants, needed money for mortgages in the 1800s, the money came from what part of the world?

153   Polish Checkers

154   Seven

155   Vlasic. (Founded by Detroit dairyman Joseph Vlasic, the first jar labels were printed in Polish.)

156   1950s. (Why did the moron throw his clock out the window? Because he wanted to see time fly.)

157   True. (No Poland existed due to the partition of Poland by Austria, Prussia and Russia.)

158   D

159   World War II

160   Europe. (Wealthy Europeans had agents in the U.S., comparable to financial institutions today.)

161   Who portrayed Millie Swanson, girlfriend of widower Sam Jones, on the TV sitcom, "Mayberry, R.F.D."?

162   Jim Grabowski, the All-American running back from Illinois, was the AFLs No. 1 draft pick in 1966. Name the team.   (A) Oakland   (B) Boston   (C) Miami

163   Does hockey superstar Wayne Gretzky have any Polish blood in him?

164   Maryanna Michalska danced her way into Broadway history after inventing the "Shimmy" and the "Black Bottom" costume. Her fans knew her by what name?

165   In terms of numbers, where do the Poles rank in Michigan compared to other nationalities?

166   In terms of numbers, where do Poles rank compared to other Slavic ethnic groups in America?

167   The Poles introduced the painted _____ to the women of America.

168   What Polish name has been given to at least thirty landmarks and cities across the U.S.?

161   Arlene Golonka

162   C

163   Yes

164   Gilda Grey

165   First

166   First

167   Toenail

168   Pulaski. (Named after Revolutionary War hero General Casimir Pulaski.)

169   In what American wars have Polish-Americans **not** fought?

170   In the 1800s, significant numbers of Poles arrived in which of the following cities?   (A) New York (B) Quebec   (C) Boston   (D) All of the Above

171   According to legend, two poor fishermen, Wars and Sawa, once helped a lost prince and were rewarded with a tract of land known today as what?

172   How many parishes make up the Polish National Catholic Church in America? (A) 25   (B) 140   (C) 630

173   In what state is Poland located?

174   In the bestselling novel Kane & Abel, which man, Kane or Abel, begins as a penniless Polish immigrant and becomes a powerful businessman in 20th-century America?

175   What form of fungus has always been a Polish delicacy?

176   In 1942, the Goldsmith Company in Chicago duplicated this tasty Polish item by taking them from the field, putting them in a glass jar with spices, and pasteurizing them.

169   None

170   D

171   Warsaw (Poland)

172   B. (300,000 members)

173   New York

174   Abel (Rosnovski)

175   Mushroom. (Called grzyb or podpinki in Northern Poland.)

176   Polish Pickle

177   The Nazis were ejected from Warsaw, Poland on January 17th of what year?

178   The last U.S. volunteer in the Polish Army left Poland in: (A) 1922   (B) 1935   (C) 1944

179   In 1747, this city was the site of the first public library in Europe.

180   What U.S. president, in 1910, dedicated monuments to war heros Pulaski and Kosciuszko in Washington?

181   In 1969, Roman Gribbs became the first Polish-American mayor of what city?

182   Steve Gromek was a veteran major league baseball player with Cleveland and Detroit from 1941 to 1956. Name his position.

183   John Gronouski, in 1963, became the first Polish-American to serve in a Cabinet position. Name the position.

184   In 1936, Cass Grygier of Detroit won the International Doubles title in Berlin, Germany in what sport?

177   1945

178   A

179   Warsaw

180   President Taft

181   Detroit

182   Pitcher. (Won 123 games.)

183   Postmaster - General

184   Bowling

185   This "baby boy" doll, named after the grandson of Archie Bunker, was the first Polish-American doll.

186   This comic strip character, modeled after a real-life Polish-American prizefighter, was originally called Joe Dumbelletski in the 1920s.

187   The "Stomil" made headlines around the world in 1986 when it arrived several days late for the Statue of Liberty celebration in New York. What is the "Stomil"?

188   The Detroit Institute of Arts is the only major museum in the U.S. with a Polish what?

189   In what year was martial law declared in Poland?

190   When was Polish-American Day first observed at the U.S. State Department?   (A) 1946   (B) 1959   (C) 1978

191   What U.S. president in 1918 urged Congress to help create an independant Poland after World War I?

192   In 1917, the Polish Falcons opened a school in Pennsylvania to train officers to fight for what?

185   The Joey Stivic Doll. (Never became a commercial success.)

186   Joe Palooka

187   A Polish sailboat. (Had a crew of six when it arrived in New York.)

188   Auxiliary

189   1981. (Ended in 1983.)

190   C

191   Woodrow Wilson

192   Polish Freedom in World War I

193   Robert Gutowski, from Occidental College, was internationally renowned in what track and field event during the 1950s?

194   Which of these entertainers is of Polish descent? (A) Buddy Hackett   (B) Michael J. Fox   (C) Carol Burnett

195   What Polish-American was a standout linebacker for the Pittsburgh Steelers during the 1970s?

196   Polish-American Ruth Handler and her daughter, Barbra, are the two women behind the success of what doll?

197   What did Marvel Books publish on Pope John Paul II in 1982?

198   What single word is given to people of Polish descent living outside Poland?

199   Where is Warsaw located? (A) Indiana   (B) New York   (C) Poland   (D) North Carolina   (E) Illinois

200   If someone called you a "Dupa" (DOO-pa), what is the translation in English?

193   Pole-Vaulting

194   A

195   Jack Ham

196   The Barbie Doll. (Ruth Handler also co-founded the Mattel Toy Company.)

197   A comic strip

198   Polonia

199   All of the above

200   Ass

201   There has never been any evidence of ancient life in Poland. True or False

202   Poland's new Post-World War I Constitution took effect in what year?

203   Founded in 1918 and located in Lublin, Poland, this is the only Catholic _____ in a communist nation?

204   In what year was Solidarity born?

205   In the early 1900s, Nathan's (as in Nathan Handwerker the Polish immigrant) became the largest and most famous _____ _____ stand in the world.

206   The first person of Polish descent to enter outer space was aboard a spacecraft from what country?

207   What church did Rev. Francis Hodur (1866-1953) found?

208   Polish-American Roald Hoffman, Professor at Cornell University, won the Nobel Prize in what category?

201   False. (Evidence found in the 1930s.)

202   1921

203   University. (The Catholic University of Lublin.)

204   1981

205   Hot Dog. (Nathan's today is one of the few family-owned fast food chains left in America, selling 15 million hot dogs annually.)

206   U.S.S.R. (Major Miroslaw Hermaszewski)

207   Polish National Catholic Church

208   Chemistry

209   The slang word "Polack" has always been an offensive term toward Polish people. True or False

210   Vodka was first distilled in Poland during what century?

211   Zubrowka is a brand name for what item from Poland, flavored with a sprig of grass?

212   If someone offered you a bottle of "Krakus" from Poland, what would you have?

213   The mass exodus from Poland after 1870 was primarily due to what?

214   Alliance College is one of two Polish-American colleges in the U.S. It is located at Cambridge Springs, _____.

        (A) Ohio   (B) Pennsylvania   (C) New York

215   The Quota Law of 1924 lessened the flow of immigration from Poland which had peaked in what decade?

216   In September, 1897, a strike in Lattimer, Pennsylvania by Polish and other Slavic _____ _____ resulted in 19 deaths.

209   False. (It was once a legitimate term, meaning native of Poland. This term even appears in Shakespeare's "Hamlet.")

210   12th. (Vodka from Poland is often flavored and aged in wood.)

211   Vodka. (The grass used is grown specially for a certain breed of bison, giving the vodka a yellowish tinge and an aromatic flavor.)

212   Beer. (A brand name beer with a pronounced barley-malt robust flavor.)

213   The Poor Economy

214   B. (Opened in 1912.)

215   1910s

216   Coal miners

217   Which man helped provide aid to Poland after both world wars?   (A) Herbert Hoover (B) J. Edgar Hoover   (C) Casimir Hoover

218   Who was the first Heisman Trophy winner ever to pass up football for a professional baseball career?

219   In 1953, Polish pilot Francis Jarecki defected, giving the West its first look at what aircraft from Russia?

220   Leon Jastremski, a former captain in the Confederate Army, was Mayor of what city in Louisiana from 1876 to 1882. [Hint: This city's name has two words and is French in origin.]

221   What television sitcom had the character "Reverend" Jim Ignatowski, a burned-out survivor of the psychedelic sixties?

222   Claire Kronski was the lawyer and lady friend of Detective Matt Helm in what 1975 TV crime show?

223   What former Chicago Bear All-Pro linebacker portrayed officer "Ski" Butowski in the 1984 TV crime show "Blue Thunder"?

224   In what 1976 TV crime show was Officer Paul Shonsk the assistant to Sergeant Dominick Delvecchio?

217   A

218   Vic Janowicz. (The former Ohio State running back played 83 games for the Pirates, batting .214.)

219   MIG

220   Baton Rouge

221   "Taxi"

222   "Matt Helm"

223   Dick Butkus

224   "Delvecchio"

225   Poland, under King Chrobry, surprised Europe in the 11th century by forming an alliance with what empire?

226   Boleslaw Chrobry (Boleslaus the Brave) from the House of Piast was the first _____ of Poland.

227   Jews in Poland were persecuted under the Piast Dynasty in the 13th century. True or False

228   The U.S. Congress, in 1834, granted a group of Polish exiles over 22,000 acres of land in what state?
      (A) Michigan   (B) Illinois   (C) New York

229   Who, on November 1, 1973, did Richard Nixon name as the new special prosecutor in the Watergate affair?

230   Polish-American, John Karlen, won an Emmy Award in 1986 for his portrayal of Harvey Lacey on what TV show?

231   Erazm Jerzmanowski arrived in the U.S. in 1875 and shortly after invented the: (A) Gas Burner (B) Coal Burner (C) Wood Burner

232   Born in 1899, people remember Ida Kaminska for her what?

225   German. (Though short-lived, this enhanced the international prestige of Poland and won independence for the Polish Catholic Church.)

226   King (1025 A.D.)

227   False. (Poland granted Jews equal protection under the law while other countries brutally persecuted them.)

228   B. (Andrew Jackson signed this bill.)

229   Leon Jaworski

230   "Cagney & Lacey." (Best Supporting Actor in a Drama.)

231   A

232   Acting. (movies)

233   In what hit TV sitcom was Lenny Kowznovski a friend and co-worker of Laverne DeFazio and Shirley Feeney?

234   What 1978 TV crime show portrayed character Martin Kazinski as a lawyer who earned his degree while serving time in prison?

235   Angie Globagoski was a female Sweathog on what TV sitcom?

236   What segment of "The NBC Wednesday Movie", from 1972 to 1974, starred George Peppard as an independent insurance investigator of Polish descent?

237   The union of Poland and Lithuania in 1385 was involuntary. True or False

238   While under the Piast Dynasty, Poland achieved very little influence in Europe during the 11th through 14th centuries. True or False

239   The 13th century was a quiet period in Poland's history. True or False

240   Unlike other European countries, Poland never engaged in religious wars throughout history. True or False

233   "Laverne and Shirley"

234   "Kaz"

235   "Welcome Back, Kotter"

236   "Banacek"

237   False. (Jagiello, Grand Duke of Lithuania, married Poland's Queen Jadwiga, descended from the Piast Dynasty.)

238   False

239   False. (Fought off invasions by Mongolia, Prussia and Lithuania.)

240   True. (Various religious dissidents found freedom in Poland.)

241   Bronislaw Kaper is best known for his contributions to
       Hollywood's motion pictures as a: (A) Stunt Man
       (B) Director (C) Music Scorer

242   What was the occupation of Joseph Karge before be-
       coming a professor at Princeton in 1892?
       (A) Chemist   (B) Civil War General   (C) Artist

243   This NFL quarterback will be remembered for having an
       arm to match his nickname, "The Polish Rifle."
       Name the quarterback.

244   After arriving in Hollywood in 1942, this man became
       known as the bald Polish character actor in movies like
       "Abbott and Costello Meet the Mummy."

245   What is the character name of the Polish-American
       son-in-law who loved to bait Archie Bunker on TVs
       "All in the Family"?

246   Max Gail portrayed what Polish-American character in
       TVs "Barney Miller"?

247   Name the streetwise Polish-American sergeant on "Hill
       Street Blues."

248   In 1834, the first Polish-American _____ was
       born.   (A) Baby   (B) City   (C) Delicatessen

241   C

242   B

243   Ron Jaworski

244   Kurt Katch. (Born Isser Kac; 1896-1958.)

245   Michael Stivic

246   Sergeant Stan Wojehowicz (Wojo)

247   Stan Jablonski. (Played by Robert Prosky.)

248   C. (Ludwik Wesolowski and other Polish exiles made
       their own kielbasa and the New York natives loved it.)

249   Wars throughout history have destroyed virtually all of Poland's castles. True or False

250   The 15th century was an age of music in Poland. True or False

251   The Commonwealth of Poland and Lithuania became a major European power under the Jagiello Dynasty in the 15th century. True or False

252   Poland was born when the Slavic tribes of the Vistula Region united under princes of the House of Piast. This happened about how many years ago?

253   This versatile comedian, actor, singer and dancer was born Daniel Kaminski in 1913.

254   What was the nickname of boxing great Stan Ketchel?

255   Roman Polanski's film "Tess" marked the debut of this Polish actress.

256   Poles won their first general municipal office, in 1891 when Peter Kiolbassa was elected Chicago's City Treasurer under what political party?

249   False

250   True. (Many of the religious compositions of this period are regarded as masterpieces today.)

251   True. (Stretched from the Baltic Sea to the Black Sea.)

252   1,000

253   Danny Kaye. (He starred in "Hans Christian Anderson" and "White Christmas" among other successful movies.)

254   "The Michigan Assassin"

255   Nastassia Kinski

256   Democrat

257   The Poles brought the Bialy (bee-AH-lee) to America. What is this?

258   This ring-shaped roll, having a tough, chewy texture and made from yeast dough, was originated by a Polish man.

259   What is golabki (go-WOHMB-key)?

260   Bitki (BEAT-key) is baked _____ with sour cream and cheese poured over the top.
(A) Chicken   (B) Meatballs   (C) Potatoes

261   The Piast Dynasty ruled Poland until the latter part of what century?

262   When Poland was in its youth in the 11th century, it waged numerous wars against what empire?

263   The union of Poland and Lithuania in 1385 was perhaps the most important act of statesmanship in the entire history of these two nations. True or False

264   Casimir the Great consolidated Poland during the 14th century by eliminating feudal divisions. He was the last king of what dynasty?

257   A flat, round, baked roll topped with onion flakes. (From Bialystoker, Poland.)

258   Bagel. (Originated around 1680 by the Polish cook of Jan Sobieski, the Polish patriot.)

259   Stuffed Cabbage.   (Usually with ground beef and/or ground pork.)

260   B

261   14th

262   German

263   True. (Resulted in a vast commonwealth and the largest state in Europe at the time.)

264   Piast

265   John Kleczka, in 1918, became the first Polish-American elected to Congress. Name his party.

266   Sleeveless baseball uniforms became the trend in the 1950s and 1960s when this Cincinnati slugger had trouble getting his 20-inch arms into his uniform.

267   What Polish-American actor was born in 1923 as Tadeus Wladyslaw Konopka?

268   The parents of this New York City mayor were Polish-Jews who emigrated to the U.S.

269   Mizeria (MEE-zer-ee-ah) is _____ in sour cream.

270   Bigos (BEE-gos) is a Polish stew consisting of leftover meat, sausage, salt pork, sauerkraut, mushrooms, apples and tomatoes. We know this stew by what name?

271   Kluski (KLOO-ski) is Polish for what homemade item served with chicken soup?

272   Chrusciki (HRUSH-cheaky) is a delicious light pastry sprinkled in powdered sugar and is known by what nickname?

265   Republican. (From Wisconsin.)

266   Ted Kluszewski. (This .301 lifetime hitter asked for
         shorter sleeves but nobody listened. So he cut off the
         sleeves with scissors.)

267   Ted Knight. (He won two Emmy Awards for his
         portrayal of pompous newscaster Ted Baxter on "The
         Mary Tyler Moore Show.")

268   Edward Koch

269   Cucumbers

270   Hunters' Stew

271   Egg Noodles

272   Angel Wings

273   In 1897, some 80,000 Roman Catholics of Polish ancestry pulled away from the Church and formed what church of their own?

274   The first Polish language newspaper in America was born in 1863 and was called <u>Echo z Polski</u>. What is the translation in English?

275   In 1773, Polish Parliament established the first education system in Europe for the:
(A) Ministry   (B) Military   (C) Poor

276   If King Sobieski and his generals had not defeated these people in the Battle of Vienna in 1683, Western civilization and Christianity would have been extinct.

277   Johnny Kolakowski of Wyandotte, Michigan gained national attention in 1987 for serving what critter in his restaurant?   (A) Fox   (B) Muskrat   (C) Racoon

278   Niepokalanow was founded by Maximillian Kolbe, the Polish Priest. It is the world's largest: (A) Monastery (B) Polish Newspaper   (C) Polish Commune

279   Jan of Kolno, the Polish navigator who served King Christian of Denmark, is said to have guided a Danish flotilla to the New World in what year?
(A) 1476   (B) 1492   (C) 1525

280   Dr. Emil Konopinski of Hamtramck, Michigan, went on to become co-holder of the patent for what bomb?

273 The Polish National Catholic Church. (Because their special needs were not being met.)

274 The Echo of Poland

275 A

276 Turks

277 B. (His $5.00 muskrat dinner appealed to Catholics who do not eat meat on Fridays. It was ruled illegal because muskrat suppliers are not government regulated.)

278 A

279 A. (No official records exist.)

280 Hydrogen

281   Uszka (OOSH-ka) is meat-filled dumplings served in what?

282   Jellied or pickled _____ feet is a delicious Polish dish.

283   Krakowska is something you:
(A) Wear   (B) Do   (C) Eat

284   Czarnina (CHAR-nee-nah) is Polish for what kind of soup?

285   A bumper sticker reads: "I'm Gonna _____ All Night."

286   In one of the most decisive battles in Poland's history, the Polish-Lithuanian forces crushed whose Teutonic Knights at Grunwald in 1410?

287   Throughout history, all of Poland's kings were hereditary monarchs. True or False

288   In 15th century Poland, what percent of the population owned land? (A) 10   (B) 33   (C) 75

281   Soup

282   Pig's

283   C. (A type of lunch meat sold in many American delicatessens; consisting of chopped pork seasoned with garlic.)

284   Blood soup. (Contains fresh duck or goose blood.)

285   Polka

286   Germany's

287   False. (After King Zygmunt August of the Jagiello Dynasty died in 1572, heads of state were elected by a direct vote of the nobility.)

288   A

289   What All-Star Shortstop of the Detroit Tigers was born in 1958 to a Polish-American mother.

290   Teodor Josef Konrad Korzeniowski (1857-1924) was the Polish-born English novelist and short-story writer known to the world by what name?

291   Thaddeus Kosciuszko, the Polish-American patriot in the Revolutionary War, is known as the "Father of the American _____."

292   Thaddeus Kosciuszko, the American Revolutionary War patriot, led an unsuccessful Polish uprising against Russia in 1794. One year later, Poland was partitioned for the _____ time.
         (A) First   (B) Second   (C) Third

293   Zupa (ZOO-pah) is Polish for what liquid food?

294   Knedle (KNED-leh) is a dumpling made of minced meat, bread, salt and sweet cream and is usually served with what?

295   There is little difference between Polish canned hams and American canned hams.   True or False

296   When Poland became involved in World War II, the U.S. was cut off from what two delicious Polish foods?

289   Alan Trammell

290   Joseph Conrad

291   Artillery. (He was the first Pole in America promoted to Brigadier-General.)

292   C

293   Soup

294   Soup

295   False. (Poland has leaner, longer hogs. American canned hams are more moist and have more fat.)

296   Polish hams and Polish pickles

297   Warsaw has always been the capital of Poland.
       True or False

298   215,000 Polish-Americans served in the armed forces in
       World War I. How did this compare in proportion to
       their number in the total population?

299   The thousands of Poles who came to America under the
       Displaced Persons Act in 1948 were, in general, better
       educated than Polish immigrants in the past.
       True or False

300   The social order of 16th century Poland had how many
       "estates" or social groups?

301   Jerzy Kosinski, the Polish-American author, won the
       1968 National Book Award for what novel?

302   What was the occupation of Anthony Kosnik when he
       wrote his controversial, hot-selling book about human
       sexuality in 1982?

303   In 1974, Polish-American Astronomer, Charles Kowal,
       discovered the 13th moon of what planet.

304   Who portrayed Stanley Kowalski in the 1951 classic
       film "A Streetcar Named Desire"?

297   False. (Krakow was the capital until the end of the 16th century. Gniezno was the first capital of Poland.)

298   Well out of proportion on the high side.

299   True. (This posed a new strain on Polish-America.)

300   Six. (Clergy, nobility, burghers [traders], peasants, Jews and the crown.)

301   Steps. (The first foreign-born American writer to win this award.)

302   Priest. (Human Sexuality, New Directions in American Catholic Thought.)

303   Jupiter

304   Marlon Brando

305   What is a pierogi (PYEH-row-gee)?
(A) Filled dumpling   (B) Yeast Cake   (C) Potato Cake

306   If a relative served you Polish schandar, you would have _____ cake.
(A) Rum   (B) Coffee   (C) Potato

307   A rolled-up flour pancake containing jam or cottage cheese and sprinkled with powdered sugar is known as a Polish _____ .

308   What pastry, resembling a jelly-filled donut, is traditionally eaten in a Polish community the day before Ash Wednesday?

309   Throughout Polish history, coats of arms were provided for individual persons as in England. True or False

310   The peasantry represented what percent of the population in 16th century Poland?   (A) 25   (B) 60   (C) 95

311   Throughout Poland's history, the nobility comprised less than 1 percent of the population. True or False

312   Throughout Polish history, noblewomen enjoyed the same rights of property and inheritance as noblemen. True or False

305   A. (Typical fillings could include any of the following: cheese, cottage cheese, potato, prune, plumb, sauerkraut or meat.)

306   C

307   Blintze. (Polish name is nalesniki [NA-lesh-nee-kee].)

308   Paczki (PONE-tchkee). (It symbolizes life's sweetness.)

309   False. (Only for wide groups of people from the same clan and who shared the same motto.)

310   B. (Largest estate of people.)

311   False. (It ranged from 7 percent to 10 percent from the 16th through the 18th centuries. Other European countries had less than 3 percent.)

312   True

313   Matthew of Krakow (1330-1410) was the first Polish:
(A) Cardinal   (B) Pope   (C) Priest

314   In 1961, John Joseph Krol became the first Polish-American:
(A) Archbishop   (B) Governor   (C) Senator

315   What Polish-American is known as one of the great jazz drummers of all time?

316   Vladimir Krzyzanowski's promotion to General during the Civil War was delayed by Congress for what reason?

317   What is kapusta (kah-POO-stah)?

318   If someone stole your kiszka (KEESH-kah), what did you lose?

319   Mazurek (mah-ZOO-rek) is a rich Polish:
(A) Pastry   (B) Pudding   (C) Gravy

320   "Babka", in Polish, means "little old woman." But to most Americans, it means delicious Polish what?

313   A

314   A. (Elevated to Cardinal in 1971.)

315   Gene Krupa

316   No one, including President Lincoln, could pronounce his name.

317   Sauerkraut, Polish-style

318   Sausage

319   A. (Covered with any one of a variety of toppings: any fruit, preserves or cinnamon.)

320   Coffee cake. (Flavored with orange rind, rum, almonds and raisins.)

321   None of Poland's peasants throughout history had independence. True or False

322   Name America's largest Polish association.

323   The Polish-American Congress (PAC) was formed in what year?   (A) 1912   (B) 1948   (C) 1969

324   In what year did the Polish community of Hamtramck, Michigan incorporate into a city?

325   Mike Krzyzewski was voted Basketball Coach of the Year by the UPI in 1985-86 after his Blue Devils had an outstanding season. Name the school.

326   Tony Kubek, one of baseball's finest players, was at what position from 1957 to 1965?

327   What actress played New York reporter Sue Charlton in the 1986 hit motion picture "Crocodile Dundee"?

328   Marshall Lackowski is best known as the leader of what polka band?

321   False. (A small percentage did.)

322   The Polish National Alliance (PNA). (An insurance company founded in 1880, it has over 300,000 members.)

323   B

324   1922

325   Duke. (Won 37 and lost 3.)

326   Shortstop (New York Yankees)

327   Linda Kuzlowski. (She was recommended by Dustin Hoffman after appearing in "Death of a Salesman" on Broadway.)

328   Big Daddy Lackowski and the La-De-Dah Orchestra

329   Sunflower seeds boiled, then roasted and sprinkled with salt, was a recipe first used by Poles during the Civil War. This is known as Polish "_____."

330   Poland got its name from what Slavic tribe of the Vistula Region?

331   A bumper sticker reads: "I'm Never too Pooped to _____."

332   A bumper sticker reads, "E.S.P. Club— Exciting, _____ and Polish."

333   If a Polish nobleman's title to nobility were challenged in centuries past, the only place he could prove himself was where?

334   Hamtramck, Michigan was named after Lieutenant Colonel John Francis Hamtramck, who fought in what American war?

335   The portrait of the Virgin Mary and the Christ Child at what Polish shrine is credited with saving Poland from Swedish forces in 1656?

336   During what century did Polish nobility reduce the royal head of state to a mere figurehead role?

329   Peanuts

330   The Polans

331   Polka

332   Sexy

333   In the Courts. (He needed six sworn witnesses to con-firm his noble descent.)

334   Revolutionary War

335   The Sacred Shrine of the Black Madonna at Czestochowa (Tche-stoh-HOH-vah)

36   18th. (This uprising by the nobility opened the door to exploitation by outside forces.)

337   What Polish-American actress starred with Victor Mature in the movie," One Billion B.C."?

338   Wanda Landowska (1877-1959), the Polish-American musician, is considered the greatest modern master of what neglected keyboard instrument?

339   In 1927, Harry Lender, a Polish-Jewish immigrant, introduced what "roll with a hole" to the American population?

340   Samuel A. Levine, the Polish-Jewish heart specialist made "Coronary _____" a household term.

341   A bumper sticker reads:
        "We Need a Polish _____."

342   A bumper sticker reads:
        "Make Poland Our _____ State."

343   A bumper sticker reads:
        "_____ Me, I'm Polish."

344   A bumper sticker reads: "Kielbasa and Pierogies—th Breakfast of _____."

337   Carole Landis

338   Harpsichord

339   Bagel. (Opened a bagel bakery in Connecticut.)

340   Thrombosis

341   President

342   51st

343   Kiss

344   Champions

345   After Poland embraced Christianity under Mieszko I in the 10th century, was it recognized as an independent state?

346   In 1608, the ship "Mary and Margaret" arrived at what city in Virginia with the first Poles on board? (A) Virginia Beach   (B) Norfolk   (C) Jamestown

347   After Poland disappeared from the map in 1795, Polish culture and nationalism also disappeared.   True or False

348   What major U.S. city has the largest Polish-American population?

349   He was born Hugh Anthony Cregg III, but his Rock 'n Roll fans know him by what name?

350   This half Polish and half Italian man played the piano by ear at four and played in beer joints when he was twelve to earn money for his family.

351   In what year did Ed Lopat lead American League pitchers with a 16-4 win-loss record and 2.42 earned-run average (E.R.A.)?   (A) 1916   (B) 1953   (C) 197

352   This quarterback from Notre Dame won the Heisman Trophy in 1947.

345   Yes

346   C. (Impressed with the quality of Polish soap, glass and pitch and tar, John Smith invited Poles to accompany him to America.)

347   False. (It actually grew stronger throughout the 19th century.)

348   Chicago

349   Huey Lewis. (He attended Cornell University's School Engineering before pursuing a music career.)

350   Liberace. (Born Wladziu Valentino Liberace.)

351   B. (He was born Ed Lopatynski.)

352   Johnny Lujack. (Born John Luczak, he led Notre Dame to national titles in 1943-46-47.)

353   What variation of dance fitness combines the polka with exercise?

354   In what polka does "Peter Piper pick up pretty Polly and dance pretty, pretty"?

355   Fill in the missing word to this polka lyric: "We're going to a good old fashioned Polish _____."

356   Fill in the missing words to this polka lyric: "Oh what a pity we are dancing and not romancing; Julieda, Julieda ..."

357   The Jewish population of Poland has all but disappeared. True or False

358   What is celebrated each year on May 3rd in Poland?

359   Ignacy Lukasiewicz, in 1853, implemented the first (A) Windmill   (B) Bottling Process   (C) Crude Oil Refinery

360   Witold Lutoslawski will long be remembered as one of the world's premiere: (A) Composers   (B) Polka Band Leaders   (C) Polish Chefs

353   Polkaerobics

354   "Peter Piper Pickle Peppers Polka"

355   Wedding

356   You're the one for me.

357   True

358   Polish Constitution Day. (Proclamation of a new Democratic Constitution by the Polish Parliament in 1791, making Poland a European power.)

359   C

360   A

361   This power hitting outfielder of the 1970s and 1980s will be remembered as "The Bull."

362   She was born Janet Nowicki, but this champion figure skater became known the world over by what name?

363   Fill in the missing words to this polka lyric: "We're gonna have a Polka celebration. You bring your friends out and ..."

364   Fill in the missing word to this polka lyric: "She likes kielbasa better than _____."

365   Fill in the missing word to this waltz lyric: "Pretty Polish blue eyes, you glow with happiness and show a wealth of treasure; a love that has no _____."

366   Fill in the missing word to this polka lyric: "This is just another polka; but holy smoka, oh what a girl in m_____."

367   Polish-American Herman Mankiewicz (1897-195?) wrote the screenplay for the movie, "Pride of th_____."

368   This Polish-American man directed the movie "Cleopatra" and "Sleuth."

361   Greg Luzinski

362   Janet Lynn. (Her middle name became her new sur-
           name.)

363   I'll bring mine.

364   Beer

365   Measure

366   Arms

367   Yankees

368   Joseph Mankiewicz

369   Ted Marchibroda, a top collegiate football player at St
       Bonaventure and University of Detroit, led the nation
       with 1,813 offensive yards in 1952. Name his position.

370   What Polish-American portrayed Artemus Gordon in the
       1960s TV fantasy western, "The Wild, Wild West"?

371   Fill in the missing words to this polka lyric:
       "Hoop-dee-doo, hoop-dee-doo, I here a polka and my
       troubles ..."

372   Fill in the missing word to this polka lyric: "There's no
       beer in _____."

373   Fill in the missing word to this polka lyric: "Everybody
       has a mania, to do the polka from _____."

374   Fill in the missing word to this polka lyric: "Never say
       you're too young. Never say you're too old. Dance the
       polka all night long. It's as good as _____."

375   Alecia Rae Masalkoski attracted national attention in
       1985 with a karate performance during the talent portion
       of what pageant?

376   What Pittsburgh Pirate became a hero in the 1960 World
       Series by hitting a dramatic game-winning home run in
       game seven?

369   Quarterback. (Later coached in the NFL.)

370   Ross Martin. (Born Martin Rosenblatt in 1920.)

371   Are through.

372   Heaven

373   Pennsylvania

374   Gold

375   Miss America. (She was Miss Michigan in 1985 and later modeled under the name, Alecia Rae.)

76   Bill Mazeroski

377   Father Kasper Matoga became the first priest of Polish extraction to be ordained in the U.S. in which year? (A) 1852   (B) 1905   (C) 1928

378   Mike Mazurkiewicz was the epitome of brutality and terror in American film but was actually a gentleman and a reader of the classics in real life. His fans remember him by what name?

379   What city houses the Polka Hall of Fame?

380   If you attended a "Polka Mass" on Sunday, you would surely see dancing. True or False

381   Besides Polish-Americans, which of the following nationalities dance a version of the polka? (A) German   (B) Scandinavian   (C) American Indian

382   This became a rage across Europe in the 1840s especially in a faster version called the galop.

383   Karol Mialowski, in 1865, led the first armed revolt in seeking independence for what island off the coast of Florida?

384   In his first experiment in 1878, Albert Abraham Michelson found what to have a speed of 186,320 miles per second?

377   A

378   Mike Mazurki

379   Chicago. (Housed by the International Polka Association.)

380   False. (It's a regular mass with the music and whole tempo of the service based around polka-type music.)

381   All of the above

382   Polka

383   Cuba

384   Light. (He bettered this estimate years later.)

385   Who authored the bestselling novel, "Poland"?

386   Red Mihalik was inducted into what sport's Hall of Fame for his work as an official?
(A) Basketball   (B) Baseball   (C) Football

387   Besides Polish-Americans, which of the following nationalities dance a version of the polka? (A) Slovenian (B) Czech-Slovak   (C) Mexican-American

388   The "Beer Barrel Polka" was written by a bandmaster from what country?

389   What month is observed as "National Polka Month"?

390   Who was the first Polish-American to be elected Senator in the U.S.?

391   When this woman from Maryland won her Senate seat in 1986, it was the first win in U.S. history, for a Democratic woman not succeeding her Senator-husband.

392   Leopold Moczygemba, in 1854, led 800 people from Prussian-occupied Poland and established the town of Panna Maria in what southern U.S. state?

385   James Michener

386   A

387   All of the above. (The U.S. has more Mexican-American polka bands than Polish-American.)

388   Czechoslovakia. (Vejvoda; translated into English in 1939 by Lew Brown.)

389   January

390   Edmund Muskie (1958)

391   Barbara Mikulski. (It was the second Senate contest ever involving two women.)

392   Texas. (This group came equipped with household goods, farm equipment, a large crucifix and even church bells.)

393   Helena Modjeska, the renowned Polish-American stage actress of the early 1900's, was the godmother of what late movie star? [Hint: His first name was Lionel.]

394   Ralph Modjeski saw his Ambassador Bridge completed in 1929, connecting Detroit with what city?

395   Fill in the missing words to this polka lyric: "Roll out the barrel, we'll have a ...."

396   What waltz is often played at Polish-American weddings while the bride dances with her father?

397   Fill in the missing words to this polka lyric: "Stop those Polish jokes and love those _____ _____."

398   Stan Wolowic is best remembered as the leader of what polka band?

399   Dick Modzelewski, the All-American football player at Maryland, won the Outland Trophy in 1952 as the nation's outstanding what?

400   In 1948, the first Polish-American to head a major American city was Joseph Mruk. He was elected Mayor of what New York city?

393   Lionel Barrymore

394   Windsor, Ontario. (1,850 feet long, this was the longest bridge at the time.)

395   Barrel of Fun

396   "Always Daddy's Girl." (Written by Grammy-Award winning song writer, Leon Zarski, of Hamtramck, Michigan.)

397   Polish folks

398   The Polka Chips

399   Lineman. (Played 14 years in the NFL.)

400   Buffalo

401   Name the only grandfather ever to win a batting title in Major League baseball.

402   Who was the first American of Polish descent to be elected Governor in the U.S.?

403   What Chicago-based TV show premiered on ABC in 1956 and featured polka music and dancing?

404   When the people of Posen, Michigan took their annual Labor Day walk across Mackinaw Bridge in 1968, Mayor Louis Nogafski tired and only made it half way. What polka commemorates this event?

405   Fill in the words to this polka lyric: "Clap your hands, stamp your feet, polka music ...."

406   Eddie Blazonczyk and the Versatones, in 1986, became the first polka band to produce a what?

407   What 1986 novelty song pokes gentle fun at Polish baseball stars?

408   Who was the first Polish-American to campaign for the Democratic Presidential Nomination?

401   Stan Musial. (With his unusual cork-screw stance, he was seven times the National League's Batting Champion and three times its MVP.)

402   Edmund Muskie. (Maine in 1954.)

403   "It's Polka Time." (Hosted by Bruno "Junior" Zielinski. Lasted until September, 1957.)

404   "Half-Way Louie." (By Ruby K. and Mary Lou with the Alpomes.)

405   Can't be beat.

406   Video. (They also shared a Grammy Award in 1987 with their hit album, "Another Polka Celebration.")

407   "The Baseball Polka"

408   Edmund Muskie (1972)

409   Who, in 1980, became the first Polish-American Secretary of State?

410   The Polonaise was a popular Polish processiona_____ during the 19th century.

411   Versions of this dance were, at first, performed only in elegant ballrooms in Europe and were written into operas.

412   Name the year in which polka artists were firs nominated for a Grammy Award.

413   The polka is as popular in Poland as it is in the U.S True or False

414   The polka originated in Poland. True or False

415   Bronislaw Nagurski, the Hall of Fame football playe who was a running back for the Chicago Bears in th 1930s, is remembered by what nickname?

416   Polish-American Apolonia Chapuliec changed her nam to what before becoming a film star in the "Roarin 20s"?

409   Edmund Muskie. (His father changed the family name from Marciszewski to Muskie.)

410   Dance

411   Polka

412   1986

13   False

14   False. (Originated in Bohemia, a former province of Czechoslovakia. Bohemians modified Polish cultural dances to form the polka.)

15   "Bronko"

16   Pola Negri. (She claimed to be the one true lover of Rudolph Valentino.)

417   What Polish-American brothers, in 1987, broke the Major League baseball record for most victories by brothers who pitched?

418   Who was the first U.S. President to visit Poland?

419   Who was the first Polish-American nominated to be Vice- President of the U.S.?

420   The Poles gave to America the mazurka, which is what?

421   In June, 1958, ABC tried for the second time to televise a polka series. It was hosted by Bob Lewandowski and broadcasted from Chicago. Name the show.

422   Salve made from what large waterfowl with a long neck was once a soothing folk remedy for the sick in Poland?

423   Karol Olszewski (1846-1915), the Polish scientist, was recognized for his work with temperature and the liquefying of what?

424   Warren Orlick not only mastered this game, he became foremost authority on its rules.

417   Phil and Joe Niekro. (Jim and Gaylord Perry held the record.)

418   Richard Nixon (1972)

419   Edmund Muskie. (Hubert Humphrey's running mate in 1968.)

420   A lively dance resembling the polka.

421   "Polka-Go-Round." (Lasted until September, 1959.)

22   Goose

23   Gas

24   Golf. (Known as "Mr. Rules," he was "Pro Golfer of the Year" in 1960.)

425   Born Eugene Orowicz in 1935, he changed his name to what before starring on TVs "Bonanza"?

426   Poland's Eliza Orzeszkowa was considered for a Nobel Prize in 1905 but was rejected because of her views on what subject?

427   Polish folk medicine once included the use of this bloodsucker to "drain infection from one's body."

428   An old Polish proverb says: "He is rich who owes _____."

429   An old Polish proverb says: "A guest in the house is _____ in the house."

430   An old Polish proverb says: "Good and abundant _____ is required for good health."

431   Bill Osmanski starred for this school's famous undefeated football team in 1937.
(A) UCLA   (B) Holy Cross   (C) Florida State

432   This Polish-American actress is best remembered as the Gypsy woman in the werewolf movies with Lon Chaney Jr.

425   Michael Landon

426   Rights of Women

427   Leech

428   Nothing

429   God

430   Food

31   B

32   Maria Ouspenskaya (1876-1949)

433   What did the U.S. issue in 1960 to honor Polish concert pianist and statesman Ignacy Paderewski?

434   Walter Palaniuk, the actor, is better known to his fans by what name?

435   An old Polish proverb says: "He who gives freely, gives _____."

436   An old Polish proverb says: "A good appetite needs no _____."

437   No Polish person has ever attained sainthood.
      True or False

438   At Polish weddings, what is used as a symbol for preservation of life and the marriage?

439   Frank Parker was a quiet but persistent star in what sport in the 1940s?

440   Polish-American, Jean Parker, was a popular leading lady in motion pictures during what two decades?

433   Stamps (4¢ and 8¢)

434   Jack Palance

435   Twice

436   Sauce

37   False

38   Salt

39   Tennis. (Born Frank Pajkowski, he won Forest Hills in 1944 and 1945.)

40   1930s and 1940s. (Originally named Mae Green.)

441   Walt Patulski, the defensive end from Notre Dame, was the NFLs No. 1 draft pick in 1972. Name the team in New York who selected him.

442   Professor Felix Pawlowski (1876-1951) introduced the education of this subject into the U.S.
(A) Sex Education   (B) Aeronautical Engineering
(C) Jewish History

443   At Polish weddings, what symbol is used to remind the couple they will have to work together during thei union?

444   Pisanki (pea-SAHN-key), one of the oldest folk arts sti in existence today, is the Polish art of what?

445   Most people are awed when given the opportunity t view the Polish folk art of painting on:
(A) Glass   (B) Stone   (C) Pottery

446   Wycinanki (vi-CHEE-non-kee) is the Polish art of :
(A) Glass Blowing (B) Pumpkin Carving (C) Pape Cutting

447   Ron Perranoski was one of baseball's premie specialists from 1963 to 1973. Name his specialty.

448   Barbara ("Basia") nee Piasecka, the Polish-born coc and chambermaid, became the third wife of J. Sewa Johnson, founder of what company?

441   Buffalo Bills

442   B. (At the University of Michigan in 1912.)

443   Bread

444   Egg decorating. (Over 3,000 years old, it started to gain popularity in the U.S. in the 1960s. Every color and design has a meaning.)

445   A

446   C. (Polish cut-outs had its beginnings in 19th century Poland.)

447   Relief pitcher. (179 saves and 2.79 E.R.A.)

448   Johnson & Johnson. (When he died in 1983, she became heir to his fortune. His children from previous marriages sued her.)

449   Edward Piszek made his first fortune in fish after founding what company in 1946?

450   Who directed the motion picture "Rosemary's Baby"?

451   On average, the Polish language will be lost in how many generations after a Pole immigrates?

452   The letter "V" does not exist in the Polish language. True or False

453   Swieconka (SHFE-son-ka) is the custom of having what done at Easter?

454   The traditional Polish Easter breakfast consists of oven-roasted, smoked kielbasa with soft-boiled eggs. True or False

455   Stanislaus Poniatowski was the last _____ of Poland.

456   Jerzy Popieluszko (Pohp-yeh-WOOSH-koh) was a key figure in Poland's Solidarity movement before Moscow had him murdered in 1984. What was his occupation?

449   Mrs. Paul's Kitchens. (He once invested $500,000 on "Project Pole," a campaign to wipe out Polish jokes.)

450   Roman Polanski

451   Two

452   True

453   "Blessing of the food." (In the basket.)

454   False. (Hard-boiled eggs.)

455   King. (He left his throne in 1795.)

456   Priest

457   The year 1892 marked the death of Ernestine Potowski-Rose, the Polish-American abolitionist and advocate of what?

458   Born Stefania Federkiewicz, this actress was the first Polish-American to have her own line of clothing.

459   Beneath the city of Wieliczka, Poland is one of the largest and oldest _____ mines in the world.
(A) Diamond   (B) Salt   (C) Coal

460   In some places in Poland, the drowning of straw figures (named marzanna) marks the start of what?

461   Which of these was once Lenten food in Poland?
(A) Popcorn (B) Peanuts (C) Pretzels

462   What opera became Poland's national opera in the 1800s?

463   Russian by birth, Polish by ancestry, the world's only wild _____ is named for Nikolai Przewalski (1839-1888).

464   Casimir Pulaski (1748-1779), the Polish-American general, became a national hero after commanding troops in what war?

457   Women's Rights

458   Stefanie Powers. (Sold by Sears, beginning in 1985.)

459   B. (In operation since the 11th century, it even has a sanitarium to treat lung diseases and allergies.)

460   Spring. (Marzanna symbolizes winter.)

461   C

462   "Halka." (Reborn in 1986, this opera embraces Poland's music, dances and culture.)

463   Horse. (The Przewalski is also called the Mongolian Wild Horse.)

464   Revolutionary War. (A quarrelsome man, he quit the army, formed his own infantry and harassed the British with hit-and-run tactics.)

465   In 1924, Polish-American Forest Ranger Edward Pulaski, invented a tool which is a combination ax and cutting tool. What name is given to this universal tool?

466   Ivan Putski developed the "Polish Hammer," which is what?

467   How many different religious denominations practice openly in Poland?

468   What state has the most Polish-Americans?

469   What yellowish to brownish gem is imported from Poland to make jewelry?

470   What alternative to Mother's Day is observed in Poland?

471   Polish Prince Michael Radziwill once owned what famous building built in 1862 at Monaco?

472   Polish-born Dame Marie Rambert founded England's first: (A) Polish Bakery (B) Tennis Club (C) Ballet Company

465   Pulaski

466   A wrestling hold. (Born in Krakow, Poland, Putski once held the World Wrestling Federation Tag Team Title with Tito Santana.)

467   37

468   New York. (Almost 1.2 million in the 1980 Census.)

469   Amber

470   Women's Day

471   The Gambling Casino

472   C

473   Father Paul Rhode, in 1908, became the first American Roman Catholic of Polish descent appointed to what position?

474   Polish-American Eddie Risko (1911-1957) became boxing's Champion of the World in 1935 in what weight class?

475   What is commonly used in place of palms on Palm Sunday in Poland?

476   Borscht, the Russian beet soup, was originated by Russian people. True or False

477   The northern coast of Poland faces what sea?

478   Poland is about the same size as:
        (A) Maine   (B) New Mexico   (C) Texas

479   Born in 1899, Polish-American Maurice Rose became a renowned general during what war?

480   This Polish-American Congressman was the chief author of The Tax Overhaul Bill in 1986.

473   Bishop. (Chicago.)

474   Middleweight

475   Pussywillows

476   False. (Introduced into Russia through the Polish.)

477   Baltic Sea

478   B

479   World War II

480   Dan Rostenkowski.   (Democrat-Illinois.)

481   This infamous Polish-born pianist had a keen interest in reading palms of hands.

482   This famous Polish-Jewish immigrant was only 4'10" tall, but there was nothing small about the way she operated her cosmetics company.

483   What country lies to the west of Poland?

484   What country lies to the south of Poland?

485   What country lies to the East of Poland?

486   Polish, Czech, Slovak and Sorbian come under what general language category?

487   Polish-born Dr. Albert Sabin is best known for the cure of: (A) Polio   (B) Smallpox   (C) Herpes II

488   What Polish-American was a weatherman before becoming the host of TVs "Wheel of Fortune"?

481   Arthur Rubinstein (1886-1982)

482   Helena Rubinstein

483   East Germany

484   Czechoslovakia

485   The Soviet Union

486   Slavic.   (Western group.)

487   A

488   Pat Sajak

489   Ed, Ted and Bob Sadowski belonged to one of 16 families ever to have <u>three</u> brothers play in the:
(A) NFL   (B) NBA   (C) Major Leagues (Baseball)

490   Born in 1785, Haym Salomon was the Polish-born financier of what Revolution?

491   What is the official name of Poland?

492   What colors are in Poland's flag?

493   Name the most beautiful mountains in Poland?

494   When you take leftover food from a wedding and complete the celebration the next day, this is known as what?

495   What city in Ohio is named for a Polish immigrant?

496   Polish-American Dr. Andrew Schally shared the 197 Nobel Prize in Physiology for discovering the production of peptic hormones in what part of the human body?

489   C

490   American Revolution

491   Polish People's Republic

492   White stripe over red stripe

493   The Carpathians. (Located in the South.)

494   Poprawiny (POH-pra-vee-ny)

495   Sandusky. (Named after Jacob Sadowski —the first European to descend the Mississippi River.)

496   The Brain

497   Norbert Schemansky was voted the World's Strongest Athlete in 1951-52-53-54. Name his sport.

498   Maurice Sendak is known as the man who put what back into bedtime stories?

499   How do you toast someone in Polish?

500   It is a Polish custom to begin Christmas Eve dinner with a thin wafer, blessed and stamped with the figures of the holy family. What is this wafer called?

501   In 1985, the average person in Poland consumed how many pints of liquor?

502   How do you say "computer" in Polish?

503   What all-time bestselling novel was published by Henryk Sienkiewicz in 1896 and was eventually made into a film?

504   Al Simmons is remembered as the baseball slugger who made what beer city famous?

497   Weight-lifting. (Born Norbert Szymanski, he won four Olympic medals.)

498   Monsters. (This famous illustrator has confessed many of his monsters are actually his relatives, as seen at Sunday dinners in his childhood.)

499   Na Zdrowie (nah ZDROH-vee-eh).   (To your very good health.)

500   Oplatek (o-PWA-teck). (Known as the "bread of love.")

501   17 (or 8.5 liters)

502   Komputery (COME-poo-tory)

503   "Quo Vadis."   (It earned him the Nobel Prize in 1905.)

504   Milwaukee.   (He was born Al Szymanski.)

505   Many Polish-Americans have simplified the surname Lukasiewicz by changing it to what?

506   Nobel Laureate Isaac Bashevis Singer is best known for chronicling Jewish life in his native Poland and in the U.S. with his: (A) Short Stories (B) Videos (C) Plays

507   Restauracja (rest-au-RATcee-ah) are restaurants in Poland categorized from 'A' to 'D', with 'A' being the: (A) Best   (B) Worst

508   What Polish word means "tasty" or "yummy in the tummy"?

509   Boze Narodzenie (BO-rze NA-roh-dzenee-eh) is Polish for what holiday?

510   A popular Lenten service among Poles is gorzkie zale (GORZ-keh ZAH-leh) meaning what?

511   What former major league baseball star, of Polish descent, was nicknamed "Moose"?

512   Polish-American Curtis Sliwa organized the national group of "public defenders" known by what heavenly name?

505   Luke, Lukas or Lucas

506   A

507   A. (Posted on the front window or on the menu.)

508   Smaczne (SMAH-tchne)

509   Christmas

510   Bitter Sorrows

511   Bill Skowron. (He batted .282, hit 211 home runs and had 888 RBIs during 14 seasons.)

512   Guardian Angels. (The group was originally known as the Rock Bricade in 1976.)

513   Jerzy Sokalski became the first Polish-American graduate of what military academy during the 19th century?

514   Gabriel Sovulewski (1866-1939) built hundreds of miles of tourist routes through what national park in California?

515   What is the title of Poland's National Anthem?

516   Older Polish-American family members with close ties to Poland will remember Dozynki (Doe-ZHIN-kee), the festival to celebrate what?

517   Tradition has Polish people attending what mass a Christmas?

518   Some of the most famous horse studs in Europe came from Poland prior to World War I. True or False

519   This man, born in Poland, produced big-budget film like "The African Queen," "The Bridge on the Rive Kwai" and "Lawrence of Arabia."

520   What famous fashion designer considered the "babushk look" for his Fall, 1982 collection?

513   West Point.   (He died in 1867 during the Civil War.)

514   Yosemite National Park

515   "Poland Has Not Perished Yet."

516   Fall Harvest

517   Midnight Mass (Pasterka)

518   True. (As a horse-breeding nation, Poland has been second to none for centuries.)

519   Sam Spiegel

520   Yves St. Laurent

521   This renowned Polish-American orchestra conductor was the second husband of Gloria Vanderbilt.

522   This Polish-American football coach led his Kansas City Chiefs to a Super Bowl championship in 1970.

523   Polish tradition has what type of meat served at dinner on Christmas Eve?

524   If someone told you in Polish that he or she had to go siu siu (shoe shoe), what does this mean?

525   On Three Kings Day in Poland (Trzech Kroli), blessed incense and chalk are distributed at church to mark one's doorpost at home with whose initials?

526   Many of the pilsner-type beers brewed in Poland are all-malt and unpasteurized. True or False

527   What actress learned Polish for her Oscar-winning performance in "Sophie's Choice"?

528   Sir Pawel Strzelecki (1797-1873) explored Australia and named its largest _____ after Kosciuszko, the war hero.   (A) Lake   (B) City   (C) Mountain

521   Leopold Stokowski. (1882-1977; His career spanned over 7,000 performances.)

522   Hank Stram

523   No meat is served!

524   Go to the bathroom.

525   The Wisemen

526   True

527   Meryl Streep

528   C

529   This Polish-American actress rose to fame under Director Cecil B. DeMille and became the highest paid star at Paramount. [Hint: initials G. S.]

530   The last name of this Polish-American actress is pronounced 'sweet' in Polish and means 'dawn'.

531   Poland has the largest free-roaming herd of what in the world?

532   Nowy Rok (NOvi-Rohk) is what holiday in both Poland and the U.S.?

533   In Poland, the children's game of chowanego (hoVAN-egg-oh) is equivalent to what game in the U.S.?

534   If you stopped in at a bar mleczny (bahr-MLETCH-ni) in Poland, you would be at a:
(A) Beer Garden   (B) Milk Bar   (C) Fitness Center

535   Polish-American Stanley Switlik was a pioneer in the design of the:
(A) Motorcycle   (B) Hearing Aid   (C) Parachute

536   In 1981, Edmund Szoka (SHOH-ka) became Detroit first Polish-American:
(A) Golf Pro   (B) Bank President   (C) Archbishop

529   Gloria Swanson. (Born Josephine Swenson.)

530   Loretta Swit.   (She never changed her name.)

531   Bison. (At Bialowieski Forest.)

532   New Year's Day

533   Hide-and-Seek

534   B. (Features a fast meal. You can choose ice cream, yogurt and drinks made with milk or yogurt; no alcoholic drinks.)

535   C

536   C

537   Miecislaus Szymczak was the first Polish-American to hold a high government post when, in 1936, he became Governor of: (A) Illinois (B) Wisconsin (C) The Federal Reserve Board

538   George Szypula dominated this sport in the late 1930s and early 1940s while a student at Temple University (A) Gymnastics (B) Wrestling (C) Fencing

539   Poland is known for "Goldwasser," a famous brand of what?

540   If you visited Poland, you would probably be impressed with the medieval beauty of Krakow, a city located in what section of the country?

541   Christmas Eve dinner in Poland has one empty seat at the table. This seat is saved for whom?

542   Christmas Eve dinner in Poland consists of how many courses?

543   Tchaikovsky, the great Russian composer, was of Polish descent. True or False

544   In 1986, actor Stacy Keach married Malgosia Tomassi the well known Polish: (A) Playwright (B) Actress (C) Rock Star

537   C

538   A

539   Liqueur

540   Southern

541   "Unknown Strangers." (The Poles say, "Our hearts are open to stranger, kith and kin.")

542   12. (One for each of the apostles.)

543   True. (His father was Polish.)

544   B

545   This man distinguished himself as a premier utility infielder with the L.A. Dodgers and Detroit Tigers in the 1960s. [Hint: His nickname is Trixie.]

546   What U.S. President, in 1946, declared henceforth the memory of Revolutionary War hero General Casimir Pulaski would be honored on October 11?

547   The "Polish Grand Prix" is the important event for what sport in Poland?

548   It has been said Polish craftsmen purposely place what in their work, to demonstrate their inferiority to God and to recognize His true perfection?

549   What name is given to Poland's group of 30 lakes of ice-age origin?

550   Which of the following animals are considered omens of bad luck in Poland? (A) Wolf (B) Crow (C) Pigeon

551   Konstantin Eduardovich Tsiolkovsky, The Father of Soviet Astronautics, (1857-1935) was part Polish. True or False

552   On June 9, 1922 Joseph Tykocinski-Tykociner gave the world the first public demonstration of movies having what?

545   Dick Tracewski

546   Harry Truman. (An official holiday in Indiana.)

47   Motor-boat racing

48   Imperfections

49   The Great Masurian Lakes

50   All of the above.

51   True. (His father was born a Polish Noble.)

2   Sound. (At the University of Illinois, Urbana.)

553   Stanislaw Ulam emigrated to the U.S. in 1935 and later contributed to the development of: (A) Atomic Weapons (B) Electric Iron (C) Air Conditioning

554   Two men from Poland requested to have their matrimonial offer to American women, be published in what national newspaper column?

555   In Poland, what is considered to be a lucky animal?

556   According to Polish tradition, it is bad luck to seat what number of people at the dinner table?

557   How would a Polish woman say "No" to a man?

558   Dzien Dobry (JEN DO-bree) is Polish for: (A) Good morning; hello (B) Good Afternoon (C) Good-bye

559   Who is responsible for giving Bobby Vinton the nickname, "The Polish Prince"?

560   Name the hit song by Bobby Vinton partially sung in Polish.

553   A

554   "Dear Abby." (These sincere Polish men were willing to marry any American women, sight unseen, in order to live in the land of the free.)

555   Goat

556   13. (A sure sign one guest will die before the year is over.)

57   Nie (Nyeh)

58   A

59   The late Mayor Richard Daley of Chicago. (He passed up the chance to visit with the King of Sweden to see a "Polish Prince" in concert.)

60   "Melody of Love"

561   Nee Janina Walasek, the Paramount actress from yesteryear, was better known to her fans by what name?

562   What man led the 1980 strikes in Poland, resulting in the creation of the first independent trade union in the Soviet Bloc?

563   If a Polish man looked you in the eye and said "Prosze" (PRO-she), what is the translation in English?

564   If someone said to you in Polish "Do Widzeniz (Do-vee-DZHE-nya), what is the translation in English?

565   Prosze bardzo (Pro-sheh BARD-zo) is Polish for (A) You're Welcome (B) More Vodka (C) Come Here

566   How do you say "Madam" or "Mrs." in Polish?

567   Stella Walsh once held 61 world and U.S. records in what sport?

568   Francis Warnadowicz, under the name of Franc Fernandez, is considered to have been a member of wh voyager's crew?

561   Jean Wallace

562   Lech Walesa. (He won the Nobel Peace Prize in 1983.)

563   "Please"

564   "Good-bye"

565   A

566   Pani (PAH-nee)

567   Track and Field. (Born Stella Walasiewicz, she won an Olympic Gold Medal in 1932.)

568   Christopher Columbus

569   Al Watrous was one of America's top _____ during the 1920s. (A) Quarterbacks   (B) Bowlers (C) Golfers

570   Rudolf Weigl (1883-1957) discovered the: (A) Sump Pump   (B) Typhus Microbe   (C) Automatic Transmission

571   If your Polish aunt asked you if you knew how to make kielbasa, how would you say "Yes" in Polish?

572   How do you say "Sir" or "Mr." in Polish?

573   How do you say "Miss" (as in Miss Dobinski) in Polish

574   When bringing flowers to a dinner host in Poland, you should bring chrysanthemums. True or False

575   Ludwik Wesolowski inspired what hard-working youngster, in 1854, to quit his railroad job in Detroit and become one of the world's greatest inventors?

576   Who portrayed Richard Gere's Polish-American lover, Paula, in the movie "An Officer and a Gentleman"?

569   C. (Born Al Watras, he won The Canadian Open in 1922.)

570   B. (He was a Polish scientist.)

571   Tak (Tahk)

572   Pan (Pahn)

573   Panna (PAH-nah)

574   False. (This flower is reserved for funerals.)

575   Thomas Edison. (Wesolowski was the first elected official of Polish descent in the U.S.)

576   Debra Winger

577   Brigadier General Wladimir Krzyzanowski, the Civil War hero, was the first governor of what west coast territory?

578   What was the nickname of Alex Wojciechowicz, the great pro football player during the 1930s and 1940s?

579   Which of the following are mainstays of the Polish diet? (A) Grains (B) Potatoes (C) Cabbage

580   When conducting business over a meal in Poland, empty your glass if you want to avoid drinking a lot. True or False

581   Which of the following gifts would probably be most desired by a close woman friend in Poland? (A) Pantyhose   (B) A Watch   (C) A Necklace

582   There is no such thing as an American-style bar in Poland. True or False

583   Karol Wojtyla is best known to the world as whom?

584   1981 marked the death of Stefan Wyszynski, Poland's beloved what?

577   Alaska

578   "Wojie"

579   All of the above

580   False.   (A glass is refilled as soon as it becomes empty.)

581   A

582   True.   (The closest thing is found in hotels or cafes.)

583   Pope John Paul II

584   Cardinal

585   What man waged a tough campaign for the presidency of the United Mine Workers, in 1969, against W. A. (Tony) Boyle?

586   Frankie Yankovic, the "King of Polka," is of Polish descent. True or False

587   Using first names in Poland is a sign of true friendship and is considered so important, friends celebrate the occasion by sharing what together?

588   A woman in Poland needing directions should <u>not</u> ask which of the following?   (A) Man   (B) Woman   (C) Police Officer

589   How do you say "thank you" in Polish?

590   If a Polish person says to you "Dobranoc" (Do-bra-NOTS) he or she is saying "Good _____."

591   What former Boston Red Sox All-Star is known a "Yaz"?

592   Polish immigrants Lipman, Samuel, and Marcu Younker founded Iowa's largest department store i 1856. What is the store's name?

585 Joseph Yablonski. (He was defeated and he, his wife, and daughter were found murdered in their home.)

586 False. (Slovenian)

587 A drink. (The little ceremony is called "Bruderschaft," as it is in Germany.)

588 A. (A woman who asks a man for directions may be seen as flirting.)

589 Dziekuje (JEN-koo-jeh)

590 Night

591 Carl Yastrzemski

92 Younker's

593   What Polish-American actress, in 1949, started a "cuss box" by charging people on the movie set 25 cents for taking the Lord's name in vain?

594   During the late 1800s Marie Zakrzewska was a pioneer in opening the way for women to enter what profession in the U.S.? (A) Military (B) Medical (C) Publishing

595   If you want to hitchhike in Poland, what should you buy at the border?

596   An American woman visiting Poland should not be surprised to be kissed where when introduced to a Polish man?

597   In Poland, it is customary for American men to kiss the hands of Polish women. True or False

598   If you visited Poland and met a doctor named Kowalski, what would be the proper way to address him?

599   Anthony Florian Zaleski, the great boxer of the 1940s is better known by what name?

600   Ludwig Zamenhof (1859-1917) the Polish-born doctor created Esperanto, an international what?

593 Loretta Young. (She collected $100 a day and donated it all to charity.)

594 B. (She was the third woman physician in the U.S.)

595 Permit Coupons. (Give coupons to the drivers when you're picked up. Drivers receive prizes for accumulating the largest number of coupons.)

596 On the hand. (He will probably kiss her hand when he leaves, too.)

597 False. (Simply shake hands.)

598 "Mr. Doctor." (Use "Mr." or "Mrs." plus their professional title.)

599 Tony Zale

600 Language. (He mastered 12 languages before creating this one.)

601   Leon and Carol Zarski of Hamtramck, Michigan wrote the 1987 Grammy-Award winning song "I Remember _____."

602   Count Louis Zborowski was the first Polish-American to participate in this event in 1923. (A) Indianapolis 500 (B) Kentucky Derby   (C) Wimbledon

603   One zloti, in Polish currency, is comparable to what denomination of currency in the U.S.?

604   When visiting Poland, do not try to match the Poles shot for shot when drinking vodka, unless you are a large drinker. True or False

605   When visiting Poland and a Pole flicks his finger against his neck, you are invited to join him for what?

606   If your aunt in Poland invited you over for kolacja (caul-AHT-see-ah), this would be what meal during the day?

607   Korczak Ziolkowski, in 1947, started his greatest sculpture in the Black Hills of South Dakota. It was to be a carved mountain and memorial to what heroic Indian Chief?

608   Polish-American Florian Znaniecki (1882-1958) is regarded as the founder of _____ as an independent social science?

601   Warsaw. (Recorded by the Jimmy Sturr Orchestra, this tied for Best Polka Recording.)

602   A

603   The dollar. (One zloti is equal to 100 groszy.)

604   True. (The vodka can be very strong and they are used to drinking it neat and in one gulp.)

605   A drink of vodka.

606   Supper. (Usually a lighter meal from 8:00 to 9:00 PM consisting of a sandwich, pastry and tea.)

607   Crazy Horse. (He worked on it for 35 1/2 years until he died in 1982. The project is still in the works.)

608   Sociology

609   Stasia Zwolinska, the actress, changed her name to which of the following? (A) Carole Lombard (B) Mary Pickford (C) Estelle Clark

610   If your aunt in Poland invited you over for obiad (OH-bee-adh), this would be what daily meal?

611   If your aunt in Poland invited you over for sniadanie (shnee-ah-DAHNEE-eh) this would be what daily meal?

612   What is the translation when a person screams, in Polish, "Psia krew" (SHAH krev)?

613   What American slang term, having a Polish twist, means to interfere, meddle or intrude?

614   What American slang term, having a Polish twist describes a drink of beer?

615   Analysts have estimated approximately how many U.S dollars circulate in Poland's black market?

616   There is little difference between fresh kielbasa and smoked kielbasa. True or False

609   C

610   Lunch. (At noon.)

611   Breakfast. (Usually consists of rolls, butter, jam and tea.)

612   Dog's blood.   (Used as a "cuss" word.)

613   Buttinski

614   Brewski

615      $2 Billion

616   False. (The fresh [uncooked] sort is milder in flavor, contains mostly pork, and needs long, slow cooking. The smoked type is already fully cooked, ranging from all beef to all pork.)

The American Heritage Dictionary of the English Language.
Boston, MA: Houghton Mifflin Company, 1980.

The American Institute of Polish Culture. *One Thousand Years of Polish History and Culture (Brochure).* Miami, FL: The American Institute of Polish Culture, 1986.

American Polish Engineering Assoc. *A Tribute To: Albert Abraham Michelson.* Madison Heights, MI: American Polish Engineering Assoc., 1982.

American Polish Engineering Assoc. *A Tribute To: Brigadier General Thaddeus Kosciuszko.* Madison Heights, MI: American Polish Engineering Assoc., 1986.

American Polish Engineering Assoc. *A Tribute To: Dr. Stanislaw Marcin Ulam.* Madison Heights, MI: American Polish Engineering Assoc., 1985.

American Polish Engineering Assoc. *A Tribute To: Erazm J. Jerzmanowski.* Madison Heights, MI: American Polish Engineering Assoc., 1981.

American Polish Engineering Assoc. *A Tribute To: Korczak Ziolkowski, "Storyteller in Stone."* Madison Heights, MI: American Polish Engineering Assoc., 1984.

American Polish Engineering Assoc. *A Tribute To: Matthew Nowicki.* Madison Heights, MI: American Polish Engineering Assoc., 1980.

American Polish Engineering Assoc. *A Tribute To: Professor Felix Valter Pawlowski.* Madison Heights, MI: American Polish Engineering Assoc., 1983.

American Polish Engineering Assoc. *A Tribute To: Ralph Modjeski. Internationally Famous Bridge Builder.* Madison Heights, MI: American Polish Engineering Assoc., 1979.

Bernardo, Stephanie. *The Ethnic Almanac*. Garden City, NY: Dolphin Books, 1981.

Boston Globe. *Various daily papers*. Boston, MA: Boston Globe.

Braganti, Nancy L. and Devine, Elizabeth. *The Travelers' Guide to European Customs & Manners*. New York, NY: Meadowbrook, 1984.

Chamber of Commerce, Posen, MI. *The Food You Love to Eat — Potato and Polish Recipies*. Posen, MI: Chamber of Commerce, 1968.

Chicago Tribune. *Various daily papers*. Chicago, IL: Chicago Tribune.

Cincinnati Enquirer. *Various daily papers*. Cincinnati, OH: Cincinnati Enquirer.

Davies, Norman. *God's Playground*. New York, NY: Columbia University Press, 1982.

Detroit Free Press. *Various daily papers*. Detroit, MI: Detroit Free Press.

The Detroit News. *Various daily papers*. Detroit, MI: The Detroit News.

Dziewanowski, M. K. *Poland in the Twentieth Century*. New York, NY: Columbia University Press, 1977.

Friends of Polish Art. *Wycinanki Polish Cut-outs*. Detroit, MI: Friends of Polish Art, 1978.

Hook, J.N. *Family Names*. New York, NY: Collier Books, 1982.

Kelly, Kitty. *His Way (The Unauthorized Biography of Fran Sinatra)*. New York, NY: Bantam Books, 1986.

Krickus, Richard. *Pursuing the American Dream: White Ethnics and the New Populism.* New York, NY: Anchor Press, 1976.

Kuniczak, W.S. *My Name is Million: An Illustrated History of the Poles in America.* Garden City, NY: Doubleday, 1978.

McNeil, Alex. *Total Television.* New York, NY: Penguin Books, 1982.

Milostan, Harry. *Enduring Poles.* Mt. Clemens, MI: Masspac Publishing Company, 1977.

National Polish-American Sports Hall of Fame and Museum. *Brochure.* Orchard Lake, MI: National Polish-American Sports Hall of Fame and Museum, 1986.

Novak, Michael. *The Rise of the Unmeltable Ethnics.* New York, NY: Macmillan, 1972.

People Magazine. *Various issues.*

The Pittsburg Press. *Various daily papers.* Pittsburg, PA: The Pittsburg Press.

Polish Festival of Detroit, Inc. *1986 polish festival of Detroit.* Detroit, MI: Polish Festival of Detroit, Inc., 1986.

Polish Tourist Information Centre. *Poland: A Tourist Guide-Book.* Warsaw, Poland: Polish Tourist Information Centre.

Renkiewicz, Frank. *The Poles in America.* Dobbs Ferry, NY: Oceana Publications.

Serafino, Frank. *West of Warsaw.* Hamtramck, MI: Avenue Publishing Co., 1983.

Time Magazine. *Various issues.*

USA Today. *Various daily papers.*

Wallechinsky, David and Wallace, Irving. *The People's Almanac #2.* New York, NY: William Morrow & Company, Inc., 1978.

INDEX   160